THE ULTIMATE
Fox Book

Learn more about your favorite sly mammal

Jenny Kellett

BELLANOVA
MELBOURNE · SOFIA · BERLIN

HARDCOVER
ISBN: 9798540037891
Imprint: Bellanova Books

Contents

Introduction

The mysterious, sly fox has fascinated humans for thousands of years. Their soft, bushy tails and cute cat-like appearance are just some of the reasons why we are drawn to them. But there is so much more to learn.

With dozens of different species spanning almost every continent, each fox has adapted in incredible ways to its environment. From the perfectly camouflaged sand fox to the fluffy, insulated Arctic fox, in this book, we will learn more about the fabulous world of foxes.

At the end, you can test your knowledge in our Fox Quiz. Are you ready?! *Let's go!*

Arctic fox.

Foxes:
The Basics

What are foxes and where do they live?

Foxes are mammals, which means they give birth to live young and nurse them with milk.

• • •

Within mammals, foxes belong to the genera (a smaller group) called *Canidae*, which also includes dogs, coyotes, and wolves.

Although foxes are closely related to dogs, they act more like cats. They can climb trees, have great night vision, and use their whiskers to help stalk prey.

• • •

Foxes are mostly nocturnal, which means they are most active at night.

• • •

Foxes have amazing hearing. They can use this to help find prey hiding underground.

Red fox >

Foxes live on every continent, except Antarctica. However, they live happily in the Arctic.

• • •

There are dozens of species and subspecies of fox. Each species has its own interesting characteristics, which we will look at more closely later on.

• • •

The most common species of fox is the red fox.

• • •

Female foxes are called vixens, and males are called tods or dogs.

Foxes are omnivores, meaning that they can survive on both plants and meat. Different species eat different amounts of each type of food.

• • •

A group of foxes is called a skulk or a leash.

• • •

The average lifespan of a fox depends on its species, with some living much harder lives than others. The oldest fox ever recorded was a Red fox at *Giardino Zoologico di Roma* in Italy. It was 19 years old when it died in 1997.

Rüppell's sand fox.

Fox hunting is sadly still a popular activity in many countries. However, it is becoming increasingly frowned upon, and in the United Kingdom (except Northern Ireland) it became illegal to hunt foxes with dogs in 2005.

• • •

The word 'fox' comes from the Old English word *fuhsaz*, which means 'thick-haired tail'.

• • •

The largest species of fox —the red fox—weighs between 4.1 and 8.7 kilograms (9 and 19+1⁄4 pounds). The smallest species— the fennec fox —weighs between 0.7 to 1.6 kg (1+1⁄2 to 3+1⁄2 lb).

Red Fox.

Fox Species

Not all foxes are born equal! In fact, there are hundreds of different types of foxes, which are divided into 'true foxes' (only one common ancestor) and other species such as South American foxes and the bat-eared fox, which only have some common ancestors.

Here we will look at the 12 different species of true foxes. All true foxes belong to the genus Vulpes. How many do you know already?

Arctic Fox

Vulpes lagopus

The Arctic Fox, also known as the polar fox, snow fox and white fox, is native to the Arctic region. It is a small species with long, thick white fur and a large, fluffy tail. Their white fur provides the perfect camouflage in the snow.

Arctic foxes live a tough life, and most don't make it past one year old, however, the most skilled ones can survive over a decade. Their diet consists of fish, seabirds, ringed seal pups and other small animals that they can find — they're not too fussy!

As they live in very cold temperatures, it's important for them to stay warm. They do this by curling up into a tight ball and hiding behind their fluffy tails.

They don't hibernate; however, during the autumn they will try to build up as much fat as possible to see them through the winter when food is harder to find.

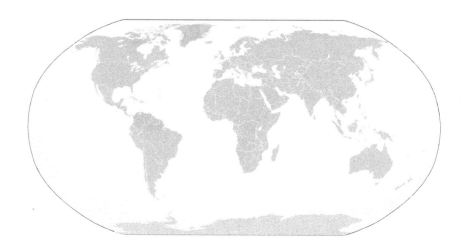

Arctic fox range.

Credit: iucnredlist.org, CC BY-SA 3.0

The Arctic foxes' main predators are polar bears, red foxes, eagles and grizzly bears.

They are the only land mammal native to Iceland, having lived there since the last Ice Age. Other areas they can be found include northern Europe, Canada, Alaska and northern Russia.

Red Fox

Vulpes vulpes

If you've seen a fox in the wild it is more than likely the red fox, as it is the most common fox in the world. It can be found across Europe, North America, northern Africa, Asia, and Australia. However, in some countries such as Australia, it is considered a pest, as it is very damaging to the native wildlife.

Within the *Vulpes vulpes* species, there are 45 subspecies, including the cross fox and silver fox, however, the red fox is the most common.

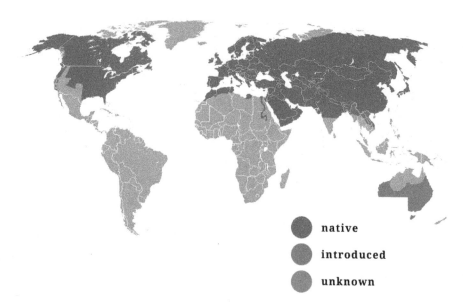

native
introduced
unknown

Distribution of red foxes. *Credit: iucnredlist.org*

In the fox world, red foxes are usually the most powerful and dominant. Other types of foxes living in the same territory may struggle to get enough food, as the red foxes will force them away. This is one of the reasons why Arctic foxes can't live any further south.

However, red foxes also have their own problems. Coyotes, bald eagles, wolves, and large cats will all prey on foxes if they get the chance.

Urban red foxes are commonly seen in towns and cities, and you may have woken up to one rummaging through your trash. They don't pose a direct threat to humans, however, they can cause a nuisance. As they don't have many predators in urban areas, their numbers have been increasing over the years.

Red foxes usually live together in pairs or small groups. Their diet mostly consists of small rodents, but they may sometimes eat other small animals as well as fruits and vegetables.

Swift Fox

Vulpes velox

The swift fox is a small, cat-sized fox that lives in the western grasslands of North America, in areas such as Montana, Colorado, New Mexico, Texas, and some parts of southern Canada.

They live in deserts and short-grass prairies, where they have a diet of grasses, fruits, small mammals and insects.

The swift fox is easy to identify by its dark grayish-tan body and white-yellow throat, chest and belly. Their tails have a black tip and it has relatively large ears.

Distribution of swift foxes, pre-1930s and now.

Credit: iucnredlist.org

The swift fox is often confused with the kit fox. They are closely related and often inter-breed as some of their habitats overlap, resulting in hybrids.

Swift foxes are mostly nocturnal, spending the daytime in their dens. However, they have been known to come out in the daytime during the winter to soak up some warm sun.

In the 1930s the swift fox nearly became extinct. Predator control programs aimed mostly at the gray wolf ended up severely harming swift fox populations. Fortunately, in the 1980s a reintroduction program started and now swift fox populations are booming and safe from endangerment.

Sadly, they still only inhabit around 40% of the areas that they used to before the 1930s.

In the wild, swift foxes have a 3-6 year lifespan, but in captivity, many have lived to be over 10 years old.

Kit Fox

Vulpes macrotis

The kit fox is the smallest true fox species in North America and lives in the arid and semi-arid areas of southwestern USA, and north and central Mexico.

It is often referred to as the North American version of the fennec fox due to its similarly large ears, which give them incredible hearing.

The color of kit foxes varies depending on where they live, but they are usually a speckled grayish-yellow color.

San Joaquin
kit fox.

Distribution of kit foxes.

Kit foxes have stiff tufts of hair on the bottom of their legs, and bushy gray tails with a black tip. You will also notice dark patches around their noses.

As they generally inhabit very hot places, their dens are very important for staying cool. They mostly come out at night, but sometimes during twilight hours, too.

Kit foxes are scavengers, so they are not too picky about what they eat, but they prefer to eat meat. In the Californian desert, their diet is mostly made up of Merriam's kangaroo rat.

There are several subspecies of kit fox, including the endangered San Joaquin kit fox. Once very common in Central California, there are now only around 7,000 left.

As of 2007, a special area in California has been designated to help protect the foxes' habitat and hopefully increase numbers.

Corsac Fox
Vulpes corsac

The corsac is a medium-sized fox that lives in the deserts and semi-deserts of Central Asia, in countries such as Kazakhstan, Mongolia and northeastern China. Although they aren't endangered, their population numbers fluctuate immensely year on year.

Also known as the steppe fox, it has a beautiful gray-to-yellowish coat, with pale fur around its mouth. During the colder winter months, the corsac's coat gets thicker and silkier with a dark line running down its back.

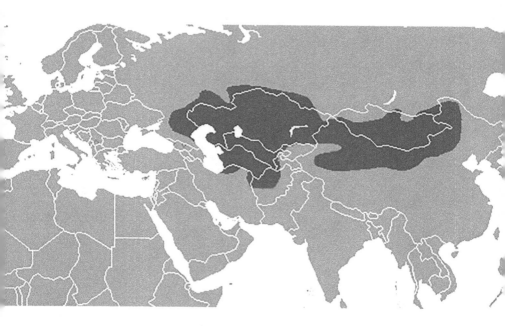

Distribution of corsac foxes.

When they are hunting, corsacs often bark like dogs, which helps to scare away predators. They may also let out a high-pitched yelp or chirping sound when they are socializing with others.

Unlike most other types of foxes, corsacs often form packs with other foxes.

Corsacs try to avoid human populations as well as mountainous areas, as they are not very good at finding food in the snow. However, they have been known to follow herds of antelopes, so they can walk in their already-trodden paths.

The biggest threat to corsacs is poachers who hunt them for their fur. They aren't particularly fast at running, so it's easy for hunters to catch them. Other predators include the gray wolf, eagles, and buzzards.

Cape Fox

Vulpes chama

The cape fox, also known as the silver-backed fox, asse or cama fox, is a small fox native to southern Africa. It inhabits countries such as South Africa, Zimbabwe, Botswana and Angola. It is the only true fox species that lives in sub-Saharan Africa.

You can recognize a cape fox by its large ears, small and pointed nose, and black-tipped bushy tail. Their coats are silvery-gray with whiter shades on their underside and throat.

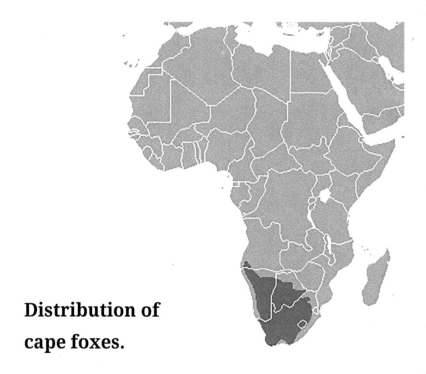

Distribution of cape foxes.

Like most foxes, the cape fox is nocturnal. It sleeps in underground burrows or holes, which it has dug out itself. However, sometimes they will repurpose a hole that another animal has already made.

Cape foxes are mostly solitary, coming together only for mating. They are very quiet foxes, but will sometimes use a soft call or whine to communicate.

If they are very scared they may let out a high-pitched bark. An aggressive cape fox may even spit at its attacker.

They are opportunistic hunters, meaning they will eat whatever they can find. Their diet is mostly made up of reptiles, small birds, rodents, insects and occasionally seeds and fruits.

The cape fox's main predators are lions, leopards and caracals.

Pale Fox

Vulpes pallida

The pale fox is the least studied of all species of true fox. It lives in a band of land that stretches across Africa from Senegal to Sudan. Its remote location and sand-colored fur that blends in with its surroundings mean few people have seen a pale fox.

What we do know about them is that it is a small fox with a long body, relatively short legs, and a long thin muzzle. Their fur is quite thin and their bellies are a lighter color than their bodies. They have long, reddish-brown, bushy tails with a black tip and a dark patch at the base of the tail.

Distribution of pale foxes.

Pale foxes like to live in dry, sandy terrain. They will move north and south within their region depending on weather conditions, as droughts are very common in the area.

They are sociable and live in shared burrows, usually with family members and their young. Their burrows can be quite large, sometimes 15 m long, and a couple of meters deep.

Pale foxes, like most foxes, are nocturnal, so they only come out of their burrows at night, or during twilight hours.

One of the pale fox's special talents is that it can retain water from its food, so it rarely needs to drink water. Their diet consists of plants, berries, small rodents, insects and animals.

Bengal Fox
Vulpes bengalensis

The Bengal fox, also known as the Indian fox, is endemic (not found anywhere else) to the Indian subcontinent. Their habitat starts from the foothills of the Himalayas in the north to the southern tip of India, as well as parts of Pakistan and Bangladesh.

The Bengal fox is relatively small with an extended muzzle and long, pointy ears. Its long tail is around 50-60% of its body length and is bushy with a black tip. Its fur color varies but is usually somewhere between gray and pale brown.

**Distribution of
Bengal foxes.**

They prefer to live in flat or slightly hilly areas
with short grasses, rather than forests and
deserts. Like many other foxes, they build and
use dens.

Bengal foxes have three types of dens: small, simple dens for quick rests, complex dens with multiple openings, and dens that they have made in and under rock crevices.

In general, Bengal foxes aren't very sociable, but they do form mating partnerships that last for many years. Some female foxes have also been discovered sharing dens with other females while taking care of their young.

Bengal foxes are plentiful but they do still face dangers, including habitat loss, disease, and predators. As they have evolved around humans, they aren't too fussed by them and are easy to tame.

Tibetan Sand Fox

Vulpes ferrilata

The Tibetan sand fox is a small species of fox endemic to the region around the Tibetan Plateau in western China and the Ladakh Plateau in northern India. They live in semi-desert areas far away from human populations, and prefer to have very little vegetation cover.

They have thick, soft coats and bushy tails with white tips. Their ears are relatively short and they have long canine teeth.

Distribution of Tibetan sand foxes.

The Tibetan sand fox's favorite food is the
Plateau pika, a type of small rabbit. Their
diet also consists of reptiles, rodents and
marmots. They may sometimes scavenge on
the carcasses of other animals such as deer
and antelopes.

Unlike many other foxes, they do most of their hunting during the day time. This is because pikas are diurnal (active during the day).

Tibetan sand foxes often work alongside brown bears to catch pikas. As the bear digs a hole to try to reach a pika, the fox will be waiting to catch it when the bear fails.

Tibetan sand foxes form mating pairs, which they stay close to and sometimes hunt together with.

They build their dens at the edge of slopes, below rocks. Their dens often have four entrances, each around 12" (30cm) in diameter.

Blanford's Fox

Vulpes cana

Blanford's fox, also known as the Afghan fox, royal fox, black fox and others, is a small fox found in the Middle East and Central Asia. It was named after the British naturalist, William Thomas Blanford, who first described the species in 1877.

The Blanford fox has wide ears and a long, bushy tail that is almost the size of its body. They have brownish-grey bodies and lighter-colored bellies. They have a darker stripe running along their backs.

Photo by Klaus Rudloff @ http://www.biolib.cz

Distribution of Blanford's fox. The light blue is confirmed populations, while the dark blue areas are expected populations.

Their habitat is usually semi-arid and they prefer steep slopes, rocky canyons and cliffs. They live at elevations of up to 6,500 ft (2000 m), and so are well-equipped for cold winters.

In the winter they have a dense, wooly coat and a thick layer of fat to help keep them warm.

Blanford foxes are very good climbers and jumpers. They have been reported jumping 9.8 ft (3 m) high on to ledges above themselves! Their long cat-like claws help them to cling on.

Their diet consists mostly of insects and fruits. Some of their favorite foods include beetles, locusts, grasshoppers and ants, but they will sometimes eat human crops too. Most of the time they hunt alone, but occasionally they will join up with their mated pair.

Rüppell's Fox

Vulpes rueppellii

Rüppell's fox is a small and slender species that live in the desert and semi-desert areas of North Africa, the Middle East and southwestern Asia. It gets its name from the German naturalist who first wrote about the fox, Eduard Rüppell.

The Rüppell fox has a sand-colored coat, which is why it is often called Rüppell's sand fox. They have large ears, like many desert-dwelling foxes, which help them to regulate their heat in hot desert climates. They also have furry footpads, which protect them from the hot sand.

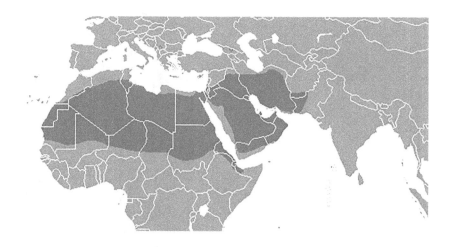

Distribution of Rüppell's fox.

Depending on which region they live
in, Rüppell's fox is either nocturnal or
crepuscular (active during dawn and dusk).

They spend most of the daytime resting in their underground dens, of which they have two different types: a resting den and a breeding den. Resting dens are usually just for one fox, whereas the breeding den is much larger and fits the entire family.

Rüppell's fox is territorial and marks out the borders of its territory using urine. A mated pair will share the same territory, which is usually around 70 km2 (27 sq mi) in size.

They live quite safe lives in the desert, with only two natural predators: the steppe eagle and the eagle-owl.

Fennec Fox

Vulpes zerda

The Fennec fox is the smallest species of true fox and is native to the Sahara Desert and the Sinai Peninsula.

The first thing you'll notice about a fennec fox is its massive ears, which are crucial for its survival in the hot desert. The large surface area helps them to release heat. Their ears also help them to listen for prey moving underground.

The fennec fox is often bred as an exotic pet, which is sold in countries such as the USA.

Distribution of the Fennec fox.

Fennec foxes have straw-colored fur and black noses, with a dark strip of fur running from their inner eye down their muzzle. Their tails are less bushy than other species of fox, but like many others, have a black tip.

The fennec fox digs large dens underneath the sand, sometimes up to 120 m2 (1,300 sq ft) with more than a dozen entrances. However, if the sand is very soft, they may have much simpler dens with only one entrance.

As the desert is very dry, they rely on water from their prey to stay hydrated but will drink fresh water if they come across some. Their diet mostly consists of small rodents, insects, lizards, birds, and sometimes fruit.

Despite living in difficult conditions, they have adapted well and have a long lifespan of around 10 years in the wild, and 14 in captivity.

From birth to adulthood

Each species of fox has its own breeding pattern. It depends on their climate, food availability and other factors – they want the best for their young.

We will focus on the breeding patterns of red foxes here, as they are the most common, but if you want to learn more about other species, it's an interesting topic to research!

A baby fox is called a kit, pup, or cub.

• • •

Red foxes reproduce once a year, usually between December and March, and give birth during the springtime. The exact time will vary depending on where they live.

• • •

The gestation period (how long the female is pregnant) is between 49-58 days.

• • •

Young kits have soft, fluffy fur, which becomes shinier and glossier at around eight weeks.

A vixen will usually give birth to a litter of four to six kits, but sometimes it can be up to 12!

Arctic foxes have much larger litters, sometimes up to 14. This is because the survival rate is very low.

When kits are born they are completely helpless — blind, deaf and toothless. They are covered in soft brown fur.

• • •

For the first 2-3 weeks of their lives, kits' mothers stay very close to them as they are unable to thermoregulate themselves. This means that their bodies don't know whether they are hot or cold, and can't control it.

• • •

During the first few weeks when the mother is with her kits, the father or kit-less vixens in their group will bring food for the mother.

When kits' eyes open after 13-15 days they are a bright blue color. This changes to amber after 4-5 weeks.

• • •

As their eyes start to open, their teeth start to grow too, and their ear canals open.

• • •

Although they still need help from their mothers, kits will start to explore outside of their dens around 3-4 weeks old. They will also start trying solid food from their parents at this age.

The lactation period (how long a kit drinks its mother's milk) is 6-7 weeks.

• • •

A kit will be the size of an adult fox by the

time it is 6-7 months old, at which time it can leave its parents and start its own life.

• • •

Once vixens reach around one year old they can start producing their own kits.

Foxes are mostly monogamous, which means they have the same partner for life.

• • •

Vixens are great mothers. They have been known to do almost anything to protect their kits.

• • •

Kits have eight different sounds that they can make. At 19 days old they start using a "wow wow wow" sound when they want attention.

Arctic fox kit in Svalbard, Norway >

Fox behavior and habits

What do foxes do all day? Let's find out!

Fox dens are also known as earths or burrows. Their dens are sometimes inherited and sometimes built from scratch. They are usually well-hidden and can be very sophisticated with several entrances.

• • •

Foxes have whiskers on their faces and legs, which they use to navigate, like cats.

Most foxes are solitary creatures and like to live and hunt alone. The only time they spend time with other foxes is when they are mating or raising their young. However, there are some less-common species of fox that are much more sociable.

• • •

Foxes are very vocal and produce over 40 different sounds to communicate with each other. A sound called gekkering, which sounds like deep chattering, is one of the most common sounds and is used in disputes.

Foxes are very smart. They can survive in extreme environments: searching for food, staying warm, and protecting their young.

• • •

Foxes have spines on their tongues to help them clean themselves and their young.

• • •

Foxes are considered to be friendly towards humans. However, they still prefer to be wild and aren't recommended for keeping as pets.

• • •

The most common species of fox kept as an exotic pet is the fennec fox.

Fox kits exploring outside
of their den.

Sadly, foxes are commonly hunted for their beautiful fur. Fox fur can be very expensive and is used to make coats, hats and other garments.

• • •

Foxes hunt by stalking their prey. They use a pouncing technique that takes their prey by surprise and allows the fox to make the kill very quickly.

• • •

Foxes are opportunistic hunters, which means they aren't too fussy about what they eat. If they can catch it, they will eat it!

Depending on its habitat and how much food is available, a fox's hunting range is around 1-5 sq/miles (1.6-8 sq/km).

• • •

Foxes continually search for food within their territory, and when they have checked a place they will mark it with urine.

• • •

Like humans, foxes have binocular vision. This means that both eyes face forward and the combination of views from both eyes allows their brains to calculate distance.

Foxes are territorial and will fight other foxes that come into their territory.

• • •

Although foxes are known for being nocturnal, in recent years it has become much more common to see foxes during the twilight and sometimes daytime hours, particularly in urban areas.

• • •

Spring is the most likely time that you will see a fox during the daytime, as this is when they are starting to teach their kits to hunt and allowing them to go outside of the den.

Foxes rarely sleep inside their dens, except for mothers and kits. Instead, they usually sleep just outside the den either in the open or under a bush.

• • •

When not used for raising kits, fox dens are primarily used for storing food. Foxes usually catch much more food than they need and then store it in their dens, particularly as winter approaches.

• • •

Not far from their dens, foxes have areas called latrines, where they do their toilet business.

If the weather is really bad or they are
escaping a predator, foxes may temporarily
hijack a rabbit, or other animal, hole to find
safety.

Foxes in Folklore and Popular Culture

The fox plays an important role in modern and ancient culture. In some cultures the fox symbolizes only positive traits, in others it is quite the opposite.

Some of the positive traits that a fox represents, include creativity, passion, charm and wisdom.

Some of the more negative traits include demonic, trickster, cunning and slyness!

Foxes, whichever way they are perceived, play an important part in folklore and popular culture around the world, particularly in Europe and Asia.

• • •

Aesop's Fables, a collection of fables from Ancient Greece, contains many stories that involve a fox. It is one of the earliest records of foxes being depicted in folklore.

• • •

English children's author, Beatrix Potter, featured a fox in many of her popular books. *The Tale of Mr. Tod* is about a fox who is the enemy of a badger.

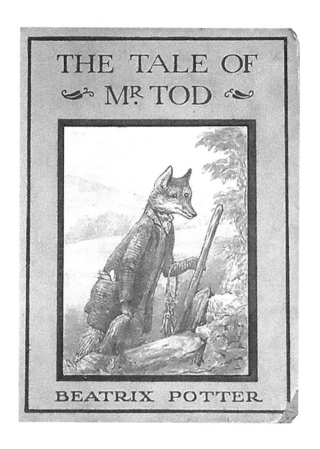

First edition cover of Beatrix
Potter's book *The Tale of Mr. Tod*.

Fantastic Mr. Fox is a popular children's book by another English author—Roald Dahl. This funny book is about a clever and sneaky fox who annoys the local farmers.

• • •

The song *'What does the Fox Say?'* released in 2013 by Ylvis, was the top-streamed music video of the year and by 2021 had over one billion views on Youtube.

• • •

The Royal Navy (the UK's naval warfare force) has 16 ships called 'HMS Fox'.

The 2007 movie *'The Fox and the Child'*, is a lovely story about a young girl who befriends a fox.

• • •

In Chinese, Japanese and Korean folklore, foxes are powerful spirits that often take on the form of female human bodies to entice and trick men.

• • •

In Chinese culture, foxes are connected with the afterlife. If you see a fox it is a signal from the afterlife or spirit realm — sometimes good, sometimes bad, depending on what you believe.

Prince Hanzoku being terrorized by a nine-tailed fox spirit, painted by Utagawa Kuniyoshi, a famous Japanese artist from the 19th century.

Some people believe that if you see a fox in your dreams, then wealth is coming your way.

• • •

The word fox is used in various figures of speech. For example 'foxy' can be used to describe an attractive, often red-haired woman. While the word shenanigan is believed to come from the Irish expression meaning *'I play a fox'*.

• • •

The Moche people of ancient Peru worshiped the fox. The fox was depicted as a warrior that used its mind, rather than physical force, to fight.

The term 'outfoxing' started in ancient Greek literature. They used the term *'outfoxing our opponents'* in reference to the cunning fox, and the term is still used today.

• • •

In some cultures, seeing a fox crossing in front of you can be an omen of good luck or that you are on the right path in life.

• • •

Foxes were an important part of Native American folklore and legends, but they were symbolized in different ways depending on which tribe you were from.

Other Fun Facts

There's so much more to learn about foxes, so here are a few more of some of our favorite facts.

Foxes are very smelly! They produce a very sickly smell from a gland at the base of their tail. If you start smelling this around your house or garden, you know that a fox is nearby.

• • •

Scientists believe that foxes are able to sense the Earth's magnetic field to subconsciously work out where their prey is.

Foxes are very playful. They will sometimes just play around with themselves, but also with other animals, including deer.

• • •

Foxes are the only type of canoid that can retract their claws as cats do.

• • •

If foxes are raiding your trashcan or bothering your pets, you can scare them off by spraying some scents that they really don't like — and it won't cause them any harm. Chili, garlic, and white vinegar are some of the foxes' least favorite smells!

Foxes have vertical pupils, like cats. These help them to see better at night.

• • •

The flying fox is not a breed of fox — it is actually a type of large bat.

• • •

Charles Darwin discovered a species of fox. It is called the Darwin's fox, and is an endangered species living in the Nahuelbuta National Park in Chile.

• • •

Despite being very closely related, foxes and dogs can not be bred together.

**Black-backed sand fox
and her kit.**

There is a star constellation known as the 'little fox'. It was introduced in 1687.

• • •

Some Arctic fox dens are over 100 years old, as they are passed down from generation to generation.

• • •

Perhaps you want to be able to identify fox poop in the wild? Fox poop usually has visible hair, bones, seeds and insects in it. The ends are twisted and they are about 2 inches (5 cm) long.

FOX *quiz*

Now test your knowledge in our Fox Quiz! Answers are on page 104.

1. What are female foxes called?

2. Which species of fox is the smallest?

3. Which continent will you not find foxes on?

4. What do you call a group of foxes?

5. How many species of true fox are there?

6. Arctic foxes hibernate. True or false?

7. What is the smallest species of true fox living in North America?

8. Where does the Cape fox live?

9. What is a baby fox called?

10. What color are kits eyes when they first open?

11. How many kits are usually in a red fox litter?

12. What sound do kits start to make when they are 19 days old?

13. What are some other terms for a fox den?

14. Foxes are opportunistic hunters. True or false?

15. What type of vision do foxes have?

16. What is a latrine?

17. What type of fox is a flying fox?

18. What genera/group do foxes belong to?

19. Which other animals belong to this group?

20. What is gekkering?

Answers

1. Vixens.
2. Fennec fox.
3. Antarctica.
4. A skulk or a leash.
5. Twelve.
6. False.
7. Kit fox.
8. In southern Africa.
9. A kit, cub or pup.
10. Bright blue.
11. Between 4-6, but sometimes up to 12.
12. Wow wow wow.
13. Earth or burrow.
14. True.
15. Binocular vision.
16. An area where foxes do their toilet business.
17. Sorry, that's a trick question! Flying foxes are bats.
18. Canidae.
19. Dogs, coyotes and wolves.
20. A sound that foxes make when they are having a dispute.

Fox
WORD SEARCH

```
F S C X Z W F R G N A C
Y Q F C V U L P E S R P
T U G O I Q W E F F C O
R R F R X N G F D S T U
D B D E E E Q W E R I T
S A S S N Z S X C F C H
Q N O C T U R N A L F G
W F B A S D G R Y H O S
S O G M A M M A L F X K
D X K J H F S E F V B U
G Z X C B U R R O W J L
Z A S D G R H J Y G F K
```

Can you find all the words below in the word search puzzle on the left?

FOXES   ARCTIC FOX   VULPES

BURROW   NOCTURNAL   SKULK

VIXEN   URBAN FOX   MAMMAL

Solution

									A	
	F		V	U	L	P	E	S	R	
U		O	I						C	
R			X						T	
B		E	E						I	
A			N	S					C	
N	O	C	T	U	R	N	A	L	F	
F									O	S
O		M	A	M	M	A	L		X	K
X										U
			B	U	R	R	O	W		L
										K

Sources

"9 Fox Facts You May Not Know". 2020. Killingsworth. *https://thebiggreenk.com/fox-facts/.*

"Fox - Wikipedia". 2021. En.Wikipedia.Org. *https:// en.wikipedia.org/wiki/Fox.*

"NPR Cookie Consent And Choices". 2021. Npr.Org. *https:// www.npr.org/sections/krulwich/2014/01/03/259136596/ youre-invisible-but-ill-eat-you-anyway-secrets-of-snow-diving-foxes?t=1625912147710.*

"Bengal Fox - Wikipedia". 2021. En.Wikipedia.Org. *https:// en.wikipedia.org/wiki/Bengal_fox.*

"Blanford's Fox - Wikipedia". 2021. En.Wikipedia.Org. *https://en.wikipedia.org/wiki/Blanford%27s_fox.*

"Vulpes Cana (Blandford's Fox)". 2021. Animal Diversity Web. *https://animaldiversity.org/accounts/Vulpes_cana/.*

"Vulpes Rueppellii (Rüppel's Fox)". 2021. Animal Diversity Web. *https://animaldiversity.org/accounts/Vulpes_ rueppellii/#behavior.*

"Rüppell's Fox - Wikipedia". 2021. En.Wikipedia.Org. *https://en.wikipedia.org/wiki/R%C3%BCppell%27s_fox.*

"Vulpes Zerda (Fennec)". 2021. Animal Diversity Web. *https://animaldiversity.org/accounts/Vulpes_zerda/.*

Can You Tame A Wolf (If Yes, How?), and Do Coyotes. 2021. "Fox Babies | Baby Foxes Are Called Kits - All Things Foxes". All Things Foxes. *https://allthingsfoxes.com/fox-babies/.*

"Top Ten Fun Fox Facts | Earth Rangers: Where Kids Go To Save Animals!". 2014. Earth Rangers . *https://www.earthrangers.com/top-10/top-ten-fun-fox-facts/.*

Can You Tame A Wolf (If Yes, How?), and Do Coyotes. 2021. "Fox Symbolism | The Ultimate Guide - All Things Foxes". All Things Foxes. *https://allthingsfoxes.com/fox-symbolism/.*

"50 Fox Facts & Secrets You Want To Know | Facts.Net". 2020. Facts.Net. *https://facts.net/nature/animals/fox-facts/.*

"Fox Hunting & Eating Habits". 2021. Sciencing. *https://sciencing.com/fox-hunting-eating-habits-7812800.html.*

"Fox Behavior - All Things Foxes - Behavior And Habits". 2021. All Things Foxes. *https://allthingsfoxes.com/fox-behavior/.*

And that's all, folks!

We'd love it if you left us a **review**—
they always make us smile, but more
importantly they help other readers
make better buying decisions.

Visit us at

www.bellanovabooks.com

**for more fun fact books
and giveaways!**

Also by Jenny Kellett

... and more!

Available in all major online bookstores

Printed in the USA
CPSIA information can be obtained
at www.ICGtesting.com
LVHW022112270923
759263LV00005B/233